MASTERING C++ FOR GAME DEVELOPMENT

FROM CODE TO PLAYABLE WORLDS

A COMPLETE GUIDE TO BUILDING HIGH-PERFORMANCE GAMES WITH C++

Contents

Introduction to C++ for Game Development

1. Why Use C++ for Game Turn of events?

C++ has been the predominant language in game improvement for a really long time because of its:

Execution - Low-level memory control empowers exceptionally upgraded code.

Adaptability - Permits procedural, object-situated, and, surprisingly, useful programming ideal models.

Command Over Equipment - Direct admittance to memory, central processor, and GPU for improvement.

Generally Utilized in Game Motors - Most significant motors (Stunning Motor, CryEngine, IdTech) are worked with or support C++.

Huge People group and Assets - Lots of libraries, instruments, and backing from the engineer local area.

2. Outline of Game Motors and Libraries

While creating games with C++, you can either utilize a current game motor or make a custom one.

Famous Game Motors that Utilization C++

Unbelievable Motor - Utilizations C++ as its center language; strong for AAA games.

CryEngine - Known for practical illustrations and physical science; utilizes C++.

Id Tech Motor - Utilized in games like Destruction and Wolfenstein.

Custom Motors - Numerous studios create their own C++ motors for explicit requirements.

Valuable C++ Libraries for Game Turn of events

SFML - Basic and quick interactive media library for 2D games.

SDL (Straightforward DirectMedia Layer) - Utilized for taking care of illustrations, sound, and information.

OpenGL and Vulkan - Designs delivering APIs for cutting edge 3D illustrations.

Box2D and Projectile Material science - Physical science motors for taking care of impacts and unbending body elements.

FMOD and OpenAL - Sound libraries for audio effects and music.

3. Setting Up a C++ Game Improvement Climate

To get everything rolling, you really want the right apparatuses and arrangement.

Required Programming and Apparatuses

C++ Compiler - Clank, GCC, or MSVC (Microsoft Visual C++).

Incorporated Advancement Climate (IDE) Visual Studio (Best for Stunning Motor turn of events).

CLion (Great for cross-stage advancement).

Code::Blocks or Versus Code (Lightweight choices).

Game Motor SDKs (Assuming utilizing a motor like Incredible Motor).

Illustrations Programming interface - OpenGL, DirectX, or Vulkan, contingent upon your necessities.

Adaptation Control - GitHub, GitLab, or Bitbucket for overseeing projects.

4. Composing Your Most memorable C++ Game Program

Prior to jumping into an undeniable game, we should make a basic C++ game circle.

Fundamental Game Circle in C++

cpp

Duplicate

Alter

```cpp
#incorporate <iostream>
#incorporate <chrono>
#incorporate <thread>

bool isRunning = valid;

void GameLoop() {
   while (isRunning) {
      // Ascertain delta time
```

```cpp
    static   auto   lastTime   =
std::chrono::high_resolution_clock::now()
;
    auto         currentTime      =
std::chrono::high_resolution_clock::now()
;
    std::chrono::duration<float>
deltaTime = currentTime - lastTime;
    lastTime = currentTime;

    // Update game rationale
    std::cout << "Game running... Delta
Time: " << deltaTime.count() << "
seconds\n";

    // Reproduce outline delay (16ms for
~60 FPS)

std::this_thread::sleep_for(std::chrono::mi
lliseconds(16));
  }
}

int fundamental() {
  std::cout << "Beginning Game
Loop...\n";
```

```
GameLoop();
bring 0 back;
}
```

◆ Clarification:

Utilizes some time circle to ceaselessly run.

Computes delta time for smooth casing refreshes.

Reproduces an edge delay (~60 FPS).

5. Subsequent stages in Learning C++ for Game Turn of events

Subsequent to understanding the essentials, you can jump further into:

✔️ Game Material science and artificial intelligence - Figuring out impact location and NPC conduct.

✔️ High level Illustrations Programming - Learning shaders, lighting, and 3D delivering.

✔️ Memory The board and Execution Advancement - Keeping away from memory spills and further developing productivity.

✔ Multithreading and Systems administration - For ongoing multiplayer games.

C++ Fundamentals for Game Development

1. Fundamental C++ Sentence structure and Elements

Prior to jumping into game-explicit programming, you should be alright with the center C++ ideas.

- Fundamental Punctuation Outline
- Factors and Information Types

```
cpp
Duplicate
Alter
int wellbeing = 100;
float speed = 2.5f;
bool isAlive = valid;
roast image = 'A';
Control Stream (if-else, circles)
```

```
cpp
Duplicate
Alter
on the off chance that (wellbeing <= 0) {
   std::cout << "Game Over!" << std::endl;
}
```

```
for (int I = 0; I < 5; i++) {
   std::cout << "Adversary Produced!" <<
std::endl;
}
```
Capabilities

cpp
Duplicate
Alter
```
void TakeDamage(int harm) {
   wellbeing - = harm;
   std::cout << "Player took " << harm << "
harm. Wellbeing: " << wellbeing <<
std::endl;
}
```
2. Object-Situated Programming (OOP) in Games

C++ is an article arranged language, and OOP standards are urgent for game engineering.

Classes and Items
A class is an outline for game items like players, foes, and weapons.

Embodiment oversees game states proficiently.

Model: Player Class

cpp

Duplicate

Alter

```cpp
#incorporate <iostream>

class Player {
public:
  std::string name;
  int wellbeing;
  int score;

  // Constructor
  Player(std::string playerName) {
    name = playerName;
    wellbeing = 100;
    score = 0;
  }

  void TakeDamage(int harm) {
    wellbeing - = harm;
    in the event that (wellbeing <= 0) {
      std::cout << name << " has died!\n";
    } else {
```

```
      std::cout << name << " took " <<
harm << " harm. Wellbeing: " <<
wellbeing << std::endl;
    }
  }
};

int principal() {
   Player player1("Hero");
   player1.TakeDamage(20);
   bring 0 back;
}
```

♦ Clarification:

✔️ The Player class has ascribes (name, wellbeing, score).

✔️ TakeDamage() capability refreshes wellbeing in view of gotten harm.

Legacy and Polymorphism

Legacy permits us to make particular game items (e.g., Foe and NPC from a base Person class).

Polymorphism empowers various ways of behaving for comparable articles.

Model: Character Base Class with Adversary and NPC Determined Classes

```cpp
cpp
Duplicate
Alter
class Character {
public:
  std::string name;
  int wellbeing;

  Character(std::string n, int h) : name(n), health(h) {}

  virtual void Assault() {//Virtual capability for polymorphism
    std::cout << name << " attacks!\n";
  }
};

class Foe : public Person {
public:
  Enemy(std::string n, int h) : Character(n, h) {}

  void Assault() supersede {//Abrogating base capability
    std::cout << name << " swings a sword!\n";
```

```
    }
};

int principal() {
    Adversary goblin("Goblin", 50);
    goblin.Attack();
    bring 0 back;
}
```

◆ Key Focal points:

✔ ⬚ Base Class (Character) characterizes shared properties.

✔ ⬚ Determined Class (Foe) supersedes conduct (Attack()).

3. Information Designs and Calculations for Game Rationale

Games require productive information structures for overseeing items, artificial intelligence, and delivering.

Normal Information Designs in Games
Information Structure   Use in Game Turn of events
Arrays Store fixed-size information like surfaces, maps.

Vectors (std::vector) Dynamic exhibits for putting away game items.
Records (std::list)   Used   for   dynamic components (slugs, particles).
Maps (std::unordered_map) Fast query for putting away player scores, things.
Model: Utilizing std::vector to Store Foes
cpp
Duplicate
Alter

```
#incorporate <vector>
#incorporate <iostream>

class Foe {
public:
   std::string name;
   Enemy(std::string n) : name(n) {}

   void Assault() {
      std::cout << name << " attacks!\n";
   }
};

int primary() {
   std::vector<Enemy> foes;
   enemies.push_back(Enemy("Goblin"));
```

```
enemies.push_back(Enemy("Orc"));

for (auto& foe : adversaries) {
   enemy.Attack();
}
bring 0 back;
}
```
✔️ std::vector powerfully stores and repeats over foes.

4. Memory The board in Games
Memory productivity is essential in game turn of events, particularly for huge scope games.

Pointers and Dynamic Memory Designation
Pointers store memory addresses, overseeing objects productively.
new and erase dispense and free memory progressively.
Model: Making an Adversary with Pointers
cpp
Duplicate
Alter

```
Enemy* chief = new Enemy("Dragon");
manager >Attack();
erase chief;//Free memory to forestall
spills
```

♦ Key Focal points:

✔ ▯ Continuously erase progressively allotted objects.

✔ ▯ Utilize shrewd pointers (std::unique_ptr, std::shared_ptr) for programmed memory the executives.

5. Game-Explicit C++ Elements
Multithreading for Execution
Multithreading further develops execution by dealing with material science, delivering, and simulated intelligence independently.

Model: Running a Different String for Material science
cpp
Duplicate
Alter
```
#incorporate <thread>
#incorporate <iostream>
```

```
void PhysicsUpdate() {
  while (valid) {
    std::cout << "Refreshing Physics...\n";

std::this_thread::sleep_for(std::chrono::mi
lliseconds(500));
  }
}

int primary() {
  std::thread
physicsThread(PhysicsUpdate);
  physicsThread.detach();//Runs
autonomously

  while (valid) {
    std::cout << "Delivering Game...\n";

std::this_thread::sleep_for(std::chrono:
:milliseconds(1000));
  }
  bring 0 back;
}
```

◆ Key Action items:

✔ ⬚ Strings run separate assignments in equal.

✔☑ Separate the string assuming it runs consistently.

Following stages in Learning C++ for Games

☞ Dominating Game Circles and Engineering - Center to game plan.

☞ Illustrations Programming - Learn OpenGL, Vulkan, or DirectX.

☞ Computer based intelligence and Material science - Carry out simulated intelligence ways of behaving and physical science recreations.

☞ Advancing Code - Learn execution tuning for continuous games.

Game Loop & Core Architecture in C++ Game Development

1. Grasping the Game Circle

The game circle is the foundation of each and every game. It guarantees that the game updates, delivers, and cycles input ceaselessly while running.

Essential Construction of a Game Circle

A game circle for the most part follows this construction:

Process Information - Handle player inputs (console, mouse, regulator).

Update Game State - Update items, material science, and simulated intelligence.

Render Illustrations - Attract the game world to the screen.

Keep up with Casing Rate - Control game speed (delta time).

Straightforward Game Circle in C++

cpp

Duplicate

Alter

#incorporate <iostream>

```
#incorporate <chrono>
#incorporate <thread>

bool isRunning = valid;

void ProcessInput() {
  std::cout << "Handling Input...\n";
}

void Update() {
  std::cout    <<    "Refreshing    Game
State...\n";
}

void Render() {
  std::cout << "Delivering Frame...\n";
}

int primary() {
  while (isRunning) {
    ProcessInput();
    Update();
    Render();

    // Recreate outline delay (~16ms for
60 FPS)
```

```
std::this_thread::sleep_for(std::chrono::mi
lliseconds(16));
    }
    bring 0 back;
}
```

◆ Key Focal points:

✔🔲 Processes input, refreshes game rationale, and delivers persistently.

✔🔲 Rest capability mimics a 60 FPS outline rate.

2. Outlines Each Second (FPS) and Delta Time

To keep a smooth encounter, games need predictable edge timing.

What is Delta Time?

Delta time (Δt) is the time distinction between outlines. It guarantees predictable development speed paying little heed to approach rate.

Executing Delta Time in the Game Circle

cpp

Duplicate
Alter

```cpp
#incorporate <iostream>
#incorporate <chrono>
#incorporate <thread>

utilizing namespace std::chrono;

void GameLoop() {
    auto lastTime = high_resolution_clock::now();

    while (valid) {
        auto currentTime = high_resolution_clock::now();
        duration<float> deltaTime = currentTime - lastTime;
        lastTime = currentTime;

        std::cout << "Delta Time: " << deltaTime.count() << " seconds\n";


        std::this_thread::sleep_for(milliseconds(16));//Reenact outline delay
    }
```

```
}

int fundamental() {
    GameLoop();
    bring 0 back;
}
```

◆ Key Important points:

✔🔲 Ascertains the time passed between outlines.

✔🔲 Smooth movement paying little heed to approach rate.

3. Single-Strung versus Multi-Strung Game Circles

Single-Strung Game Circle

In little games, everything runs in a single string:

Process Information
Update Rationale
Render Casing

◆ Issue: In the event that an update takes too lengthy, the entire game dials back.

Multi-Strung Game Circle (Upgraded for Execution)

To further develop execution, we can run separate strings for:

Delivering
Physical science and artificial intelligence
Organizing
Model: Running Material science in a Different String
cpp
Duplicate
Alter

```cpp
#incorporate <iostream>
#incorporate <thread>

void PhysicsUpdate() {
  while (valid) {
    std::cout << "Refreshing Physics...\n";

std::this_thread::sleep_for(std::chrono::milliseconds(30));
  }
}

int principal() {
```

```cpp
    std::thread
physicsThread(PhysicsUpdate);
    physicsThread.detach();//Permit  it  to
freely run

    while (valid) {
        std::cout << "Delivering Frame...\n";

std::this_thread::sleep_for(std::chrono::mi
lliseconds(16));
    }
    bring 0 back;
}
```

◆ Key Important points:

✔☐ Runs material science independently from delivering for better execution.

✔☐ Guarantees smooth casing rates even with complex material science estimations.

4. Game Circle Varieties

Fixed Time Step (Utilized in Material science Motors)

In games with physical science, refreshing at fixed stretches (not variable FPS) guarantees dependability.

```cpp
Duplicate
Alter
const float fixedDeltaTime = 0.016f;//16ms per update (60 updates each second)
float accumulatedTime = 0.0f;

void GameLoop() {
  auto lastTime = std::chrono::high_resolution_clock::now();

  while (valid) {
    auto currentTime = std::chrono::high_resolution_clock::now();
    std::chrono::duration<float> deltaTime = currentTime - lastTime;
    lastTime = currentTime;

    accumulatedTime += deltaTime.count();
```

```
    while      (accumulatedTime      >=
fixedDeltaTime) {
        Update();
        accumulatedTime           -        =
fixedDeltaTime;
    }

    Render();
  }
}
```

✔️   Guarantees material science refreshes happen reliably.

✔️ Forestalls capricious material science conduct at various edge rates.

5. Game Engineering and Parts

Undeniable Level Game Engineering

A game is ordinarily organized in the accompanying manner:

Component	Responsibility
Game Loop	Controls generally match-up execution.
Input System	Handles player controls (console, mouse, regulator).

Designs Engine   Renders objects, UI, and impacts.

Material science Engine   Simulates development, impacts, gravity.

Simulated intelligence   System Controls adversary conduct and direction.

Sound Engine Manages music, audio effects, and spatial sound.

Organizing System   Handles multiplayer correspondence (if material).

6. Executing a Secluded Game Engineering

A very much organized C++ game venture ought to be measured, making it more straightforward to make due.

Game Supervisor Class Model
cpp
Duplicate
Alter

```
#incorporate <iostream>

class Game {
public:
    bool isRunning;
```

```cpp
Game() : isRunning(true) {}

void Run() {
  while (isRunning) {
    ProcessInput();
    Update();
    Render();
  }
}

private:
  void ProcessInput() { std::cout << "Handling Input...\n"; }
  void Update() { std::cout << "Refreshing Game State...\n"; }
  void Render() { std::cout << "Rendering...\n"; }
};

int fundamental() {
  Game;
  game.Run();
  bring 0 back;
}
```
◆ Key Important points:

✔🗆 Exemplifies game rationale in a Game class.

✔🗆 Coordinated into ProcessInput(), Update(), and Render().

End and Subsequent stages

☞ Delta Time and Fixed Time Steps - Fundamental for smooth development.

☞ Multi-Stringing - Further develops execution for material science and delivering.

☞ Particular Plan - Makes the code adaptable and simple to make due.

Then, you should investigate illustrations programming (OpenGL, DirectX, Vulkan) or simulated intelligence and physical science motors to improve your game further. 🎮

Graphics Programming with C++ for Game Development

1. Prologue to Illustrations Programming

Designs programming in C++ is the underpinning of delivering 2D and 3D items in games. It includes:

✔ Utilizing a Designs Programming interface like OpenGL, DirectX, or Vulkan.

✔ Figuring out delivering pipelines for proficient drawing.

✔ Executing shaders to control lighting and impacts.

✔ Taking care of surfaces, models, and activitys.

Famous Designs APIs

API	Platform	Best For
OpenGL	Cross-Platform	General Reason 3D and 2D Games
DirectX	Windows/Xbox	High-Execution Designs
Vulkan	Cross-Platform	Advanced, Low-Level Control
SFML	Cross-Platform	Simple 2D Designs and Mixed media

2. Setting Up a Designs Programming interface in C++

Utilizing OpenGL with GLFW (Cross-Stage)

♦ OpenGL is generally utilized for delivering in light of the fact that it's cross-stage and strong.

Introducing Conditions:

1▢ ▪ Introduce GLFW (window creation) and Happy (OpenGL loader).

2▢ ▪ Incorporate OpenGL libraries:

Windows: Use - lopengl32 - lglfw3 during arrangement.

Linux: Introduce with sudo well-suited introduce libglfw3-dev.

Making a Window with OpenGL and GLFW

cpp

Duplicate

Alter

```
#incorporate <GLFW/glfw3.h>
#incorporate <iostream>

int fundamental() {
```

```
// Instate GLFW
if (!glfwInit()) {
    std::cerr << "Neglected to instate GLFW\n";
    return - 1;
}

// Make a Window
GLFWwindow* window = glfwCreateWindow(800, 600, "OpenGL Window", Invalid, Invalid);
in the event that (!window) {
    std::cerr << "Neglected to make GLFW window\n";
    glfwTerminate();
    return - 1;
}


glfwMakeContextCurrent(window);//Make OpenGL setting current

// Fundamental circle
while (!glfwWindowShouldClose(window)) {
```

```
glClear(GL_COLOR_BUFFER_BIT);//Clear
the screen

    glfwSwapBuffers(window);//Trade
cushions
    glfwPollEvents();//Handle        client
inputs
  }

  // Cleanup
  glfwDestroyWindow(window);
  glfwTerminate();
  bring 0 back;
}
```

✔☐ Makes an OpenGL window with GLFW.

✔☐ Handles client info and trades cradles for smooth delivering.

3. Delivering Nuts and bolts in OpenGL

Attracting a Triangle OpenGL

Designs in OpenGL use vertices and shaders to deliver objects.

Vertex Shader (triangle.vert)

glsl
Duplicate
Alter
#rendition 330 center
design (area = 0) in vec3 aPos;
void principal() {
   gl_Position = vec4(aPos, 1.0);
}
Piece Shader (triangle.frag)
glsl
Duplicate
Alter
#rendition 330 center
out vec4 FragColor;
void principal() {
   FragColor   =   vec4(1.0,   0.5,   0.2,
1.0);//Orange tone
}
C++ Code to Deliver a Triangle
cpp
Duplicate
Alter
#incorporate <GL/glew.h>
#incorporate <GLFW/glfw3.h>

// Characterize vertices for the triangle

```
float vertices[] = {
   0.0f, 0.5f, 0.0f,//Top
  -0.5f, - 0.5f, 0.0f,//Left
   0.5f, - 0.5f, 0.0f//Right
};

int principal() {
  // Instate OpenGL and GLFW
  glfwInit();
  GLFWwindow*          window          =
glfwCreateWindow(800, 600, "Triangle",
Invalid, Invalid);
  glfwMakeContextCurrent(window);

  glewInit();//Burden          OpenGL
capabilities

  // Make and tie a Vertex Exhibit Item
(VAO)
  unsigned int VAO, VBO;
  glGenVertexArrays(1, &VAO);
  glGenBuffers(1, &VBO);

  glBindVertexArray(VAO);
  glBindBuffer(GL_ARRAY_BUFFER,
VBO);
```

```
  glBufferData(GL_ARRAY_BUFFER,
sizeof(vertices),                vertices,
GL_STATIC_DRAW);

  glVertexAttribPointer(0, 3, GL_FLOAT,
GL_FALSE, 3 * sizeof(float), (void*)0);
  glEnableVertexAttribArray(0);

  while
(!glfwWindowShouldClose(window)) {
    glClear(GL_COLOR_BUFFER_BIT);

glUseProgram(shaderProgram);//Utili
ze your ordered shaders
    glBindVertexArray(VAO);
    glDrawArrays(GL_TRIANGLES, 0, 3);
    glfwSwapBuffers(window);
    glfwPollEvents();
  }

  glfwTerminate();
  bring 0 back;
}
```

✔ Makes and delivers a triangle utilizing shaders.

✔ ▢ Utilizes a vertex exhibit object (VAO) for productivity.

4. 2D Game Advancement with SFML

In the event that you're making 2D games, SFML (Straightforward and Quick Media Library) is an extraordinary decision.

Introducing SFML (Windows/Linux)
sh
Duplicate
Alter
sudo adept introduce libsfml-dev
or on the other hand

Download SFML from https://www.sfml-dev.org/
Connect with - lsfml-designs - lsfml-window - lsfml-framework.
Making a 2D Game Window with SFML
cpp
Duplicate
Alter

```
#incorporate <SFML/Graphics.hpp>

int primary() {
```

```
    sf::RenderWindow
window(sf::VideoMode(800, 600), "SFML
Window");

    while (window.isOpen()) {
        sf::Event occasion;
        while (window.pollEvent(event)) {
            if (event.type == sf::Event::Closed)
                window.close();
        }

        window.clear(sf::Color::Black);
        window.display();
    }

    bring 0 back;
}
```

✔️ **Handles input occasions and delivers a basic window.**

5. High level Designs Ideas

◆ Surfaces and Sprites - Apply pictures to objects utilizing surface planning.

◆ Lighting and Concealing - Use shaders for reasonable lighting.

◆ 3D Models - Burden and render models utilizing Assimp.

◆ Material science Coordination - Use Box2D (2D) or Projectile (3D) for reasonable development.

6. Picking the Right Illustrations Library for Your Game

Goal   Best Decision

2D Games (Simple)   SFML, SDL

3D Games   OpenGL, DirectX, Vulkan

AAA Game Engines   Unreal Motor (C++), Solidarity (C#)

Cross-Stage GraphicsOpenGL, Vulkan

7. Following stages in Illustrations Programming

🚀 Ace Shaders - Learn GLSL for custom impacts.

🚀 Investigate Game Motors - Utilize Unbelievable Motor for excellent games.

🚀 Work with Physical science - Incorporate Shot Physical science for sensible movement.

Physics & Collision Detection in C++ Game Development

1. Prologue to Game Material science

Material science in games makes objects move, impact, and connect everything being equal. A physical science motor handles:

✔️ Unbending Body Elements - Recreates strong articles.

✔️ Crash Location - Distinguishes when items contact.

✔️ Impact Reaction - Works out what occurs after a crash.

✔️ Powers and Gravity - Recreates regular development.

Famous Physical science Motors

Engine	Best For	Language
Box2D	2D Material science (Platformers, Hierarchical Games)	C++
Chipmunk2D	Lightweight 2D Physics	C
Shot Physics	3D Physical science (Unbending Bodies, Vehicles)	C++
PhysX	AAA Games (Utilized in Unbelievable Engine)	C++

2. Executing Fundamental Material science in C++

We should begin with Newton's Regulations to move objects in a 2D space.

Speed and Speed increase in a Straightforward Physical science Item
cpp
Duplicate
Alter

```cpp
#incorporate <iostream>

class PhysicsObject {
public:
    float x, y;//Position
    float vx, vy;//Speed
    float hatchet, ay;//Speed increase

    PhysicsObject() : x(0), y(0), vx(0), vy(0), ax(0), ay(- 9.8f) {}//Gravity applied

    void Update(float deltaTime) {
        vx += hatchet * deltaTime;
        vy += ay * deltaTime;
        x += vx * deltaTime;
```

```cpp
    y += vy * deltaTime;
  }

  void PrintPosition() {
    std::cout << "Position: (" << x << ", "
<< y << ")\n";
  }
};

int fundamental() {
  PhysicsObject obj;
  float deltaTime = 0.016f;//Reproducing
60 FPS

  for (int I = 0; I < 100; ++i) {//Reproduce
100 casings
    obj.Update(deltaTime);
    obj.PrintPosition();
  }

  bring 0 back;
}
```

✔ ⬚ Applies speed increase (gravity) over the long haul.

✔ ⬚ Refreshes speed and position per outline.

3. Impact Location in 2D

3.1 AABB (Pivot Adjusted Bouncing Box) Crash

AABB checks if two square shapes (hitboxes) cross-over.

AABB Crash Capability
cpp
Duplicate
Alter

```cpp
struct AABB {
   float x, y, width, level;

   bool IsColliding(const AABB& other) {
      return (x < other.x + other.width &&
          x + width > other.x &&
          y < other.y + other.height &&
          y + level > other.y);
   }
};
```

Involving AABB Impact in a Game Circle
cpp
Duplicate
Alter

```cpp
#incorporate <iostream>
```

```cpp
int principal() {
  AABB player = {0, 0, 50, 50};
  AABB adversary = {30, 30, 50, 50};

  if (player.IsColliding(enemy)) {
    std::cout << "Impact Detected!\n";
  } else {
    std::cout << "No Collision.\n";
  }

  bring 0 back;
}
```

✔ ⬚ Works for rectangular articles.

✔ ⬚ Quick and proficient for 2D games.

3.2 Circle Impact (For Round Items)

For circles, we actually take a look at the distance between focuses.

Circle Crash Capability
cpp
Duplicate
Alter
#incorporate <cmath>

```cpp
struct Circle {
  float x, y, span;

  bool IsColliding(const Circle& other) {
    float dx = x - other.x;
    float dy = y - other.y;
    float distance = sqrt(dx * dx + dy * dy);
    return distance < (range + other.radius);
  }
};
```

✔️ Extraordinary for shots, shots, and round objects.

4. Impact Reaction

When an impact is recognized, we handle the reaction.

Versatile Impact (Bobbing Impact)
cpp
Duplicate
Alter

```cpp
void ResolveCollision(PhysicsObject& obj1, PhysicsObject& obj2) {
  float tempVx = obj1.vx;
```

```
    float tempVy = obj1.vy;
    obj1.vx = obj2.vx;
    obj1.vy = obj2.vy;
    obj2.vx = tempVx;
    obj2.vy = tempVy;
}
```
✔ ⬜ Trades speeds to mimic skipping.

5. Involving Box2D for 2D Physical science

Box2D is a streamlined physical science motor utilized in numerous 2D games.

Introducing Box2D
Download from https://box2d.org/
Interface with - lbox2d during accumulation.
Fundamental Box2D Model (Falling Article)
cpp
Duplicate
Alter
```cpp
#incorporate <Box2D/Box2D.h>
#incorporate <iostream>

int fundamental() {
```

```cpp
b2Vec2 gravity(0.0f, - 9.8f);
b2World world(gravity);

// Characterize ground
b2BodyDef groundBodyDef;
groundBodyDef.position.Set(0.0f,         -
10.0f);
b2Body*         groundBody         =
world.CreateBody(&groundBodyDef);

// Characterize falling article
b2BodyDef bodyDef;
bodyDef.type = b2_dynamicBody;
bodyDef.position.Set(0.0f, 10.0f);
b2Body*             body             =
world.CreateBody(&bodyDef);

// Run reenactment for 60 stages
for (int I = 0; I < 60; ++i) {
  world.Step(1.0f/60.0f, 6, 2);
  std::cout << "Article  Position: " <<
body->GetPosition().y << "\n";
}

bring 0 back;
}
```

✔️ Mimics gravity and item development.

✔️ Handles crash and physical science effectively.

6. 3D Physical science with Slug Physical science

Slug is utilized in Unbelievable Motor, Blender, and numerous 3D games.

Introducing Slug Material science
Download from https://pybullet.org/wordpress/
Connect with - lBulletDynamics - lBulletCollision - lLinearMath.
Essential Shot Material science Model (Falling Solid shape)
cpp
Duplicate
Alter

```cpp
#incorporate <btBulletDynamicsCommon.h>
#incorporate <iostream>

int principal() {
    // Shot world arrangement
```

```
btDefaultCollisionConfiguration
collisionConfig;
btCollisionDispatcher
dispatcher(&collisionConfig);
btBroadphaseInterface* broadphase =
new btDbvtBroadphase();
btSequentialImpulseConstraintSolver
solver;
btDiscreteDynamicsWorld
world(&dispatcher, broadphase, &solver,
&collisionConfig);
world.setGravity(btVector3(0, - 9.8, 0));

// Characterize a falling 3D shape
btCollisionShape*    shape    =    new
btBoxShape(btVector3(1, 1, 1));
btDefaultMotionState*   motionState   =
new
btDefaultMotionState(btTransform(btQua
ternion(0, 0, 0, 1), btVector3(0, 10, 0)));

btRigidBody::btRigidBodyConstructionInf
o bodyInfo(1.0f, motionState, shape);
btRigidBody*    body    =    new
btRigidBody(bodyInfo);
world.addRigidBody(body);
```

```
// Reenact 60 casings
for (int I = 0; I < 60; ++i) {
    world.stepSimulation(1.0f/60.0f);
    btTransform trans;
    body->getMotionState()-
>getWorldTransform(trans);
    std::cout << "Shape Position: " <<
trans.getOrigin().getY() << "\n";
  }

  bring 0 back;
}
```

✔️ Reenacts sensible 3D physical science.

✔️ Utilized in business games and reproductions.

7. Outline and Subsequent stages

☞ AABB and Circle Impacts - For straightforward crash identification.

☞ Box2D (2D) and Shot (3D) - Industry-standard physical science motors.

☞ Flexible Crashes and Gravity - Further develops authenticity.

Artificial Intelligence in Games with C++

Game man-made intelligence brings NPCs (Non-Player Characters) to life by causing them to respond cleverly to the player and the game world. Artificial intelligence in games varies from true simulated intelligence — it's streamlined for the sake of entertainment, somewhat flawed direction.

1. Key computer based intelligence Ideas in Game Turn of events

✔ Pathfinding - Makes NPCs move consistently.

✔ Direction - Picks activities (e.g., assault or escape).

✔ Limited State Machines (FSMs) - Basic however compelling simulated intelligence rationale.

✔ Conduct Trees - Further developed, particular artificial intelligence for complex choices.

✔ AI (ML) in Games - Utilized in present day artificial intelligence based adversaries.

2. Basic artificial intelligence: Arbitrary Development

Fundamental artificial intelligence can move a NPC haphazardly.

```cpp
Duplicate
Alter
#incorporate <iostream>
#incorporate <cstdlib>
#incorporate <ctime>

class NPC {
public:
  int x, y;

  NPC() : x(0), y(0) {
    std::srand(std::time(nullptr));
  }

  void MoveRandomly() {
```

```cpp
    int bearing = std::rand() % 4;//0 =
Up, 1 = Down, 2 = Left, 3 = Right
    switch (heading) {
      case 0: y++; break;//Move up
      case 1: y- - ; break;//Drop down
      case 2: x- - ; break;//Move left
      case 3: x++; break;//Move right
    }
    std::cout << "NPC moved to (" << x <<
", " << y << ")\n";
  }
};

int primary() {
  Npc;
  for (int I = 0; I < 10; i++) {
    npc.MoveRandomly();
  }
  bring 0 back;
}
```

✔ Moves arbitrarily each edge (great for basic adversary conduct).

3. Limited State Machines (FSMs)

FSMs are not difficult to execute and control computer based intelligence state advances.

Model: Adversary with Watch and Pursue States
cpp
Duplicate
Alter

```cpp
#incorporate <iostream>

enum class AIState { Watch, Pursue };

class Adversary {
private:
    AIState state;
public:
    Adversary() : state(AIState::PATROL) {}

    void Update(bool seesPlayer) {
        switch (state) {
            case AIState::PATROL:
                std::cout << "Adversary is patrolling...\n";
```

```
        on     the    off    chance    that
(seesPlayer) state = AIState::CHASE;
        break;
      case AIState::CHASE:
        std::cout    <<    "Adversary    is
pursuing the player!\n";
        on     the    off    chance    that
(!seesPlayer) state = AIState::PATROL;
        break;
    }
  }
};

int fundamental() {
  Adversary foe;
  enemy.Update(false);//Watching
  enemy.Update(true);//Sees        player,
begins pursuing
  enemy.Update(false);//Loses player,
back to watch
}
```

✔ **Watches until the player is recognized, then pursues.**

✔ Productive for man-made intelligence conduct control.

4. Pathfinding with An Algorithm*

Pathfinding makes simulated intelligence move cleverly from point A to B.

A* (A-Star) finds the briefest way utilizing a heuristic capability.

A Calculation Explanation*

1️⃣ ▪ Assesses neighbor hubs in view of cost (distance).

2️⃣ ▪ Picks the briefest way to the objective.

3️⃣ ▪ Dodges obstructions productively.

Fundamental An Execution in C++*

```cpp
Duplicate
Alter
#incorporate <iostream>
#incorporate <queue>
#incorporate <vector>
#incorporate <cmath>

struct Hub {
    int x, y, cost;
    bool operator>(const Node& other)
const { return cost > other.cost; }
```

```cpp
};

int Heuristic(int x1, int y1, int x2, int y2) {
  return std::abs(x1 - x2) + std::abs(y1 -
y2);
}

void AStar(int startX, int startY, int goalX,
int goalY) {
  std::priority_queue<Node,
std::vector<Node>,   std::greater<Node>>
openSet;
  openSet.push({startX, startY, 0});

  while (!openSet.empty()) {
    Hub current = openSet.top();
    openSet.pop();

    if (current.x == goalX && current.y ==
goalY) {
      std::cout << "Way found to (" <<
goalX << ", " << goalY << ")\n";
      return;
    }
```

```
    openSet.push({current.x    +    1,
current.y,    current.cost    +    1    +
Heuristic(current.x + 1, current.y, goalX,
goalY)});
    openSet.push({current.x    -    1,
current.y,    current.cost    +    1    +
Heuristic(current.x - 1, current.y, goalX,
goalY)});
    openSet.push({current.x, current.y +
1, current.cost + 1 + Heuristic(current.x,
current.y + 1, goalX, goalY)});
    openSet.push({current.x, current.y
-    1,    current.cost    +    1    +
Heuristic(current.x,    current.y    -    1,
goalX, goalY)});
  }
}

int fundamental() {
  AStar(0, 0, 5, 5);
}
```

✔ Proficiently tracks down the briefest way.

✔ Utilized in NPC route, foe development, and RTS games.

62 | P a g e

5. Conduct Trees (High level man-made intelligence Rationale)

Conduct Trees (BTs) structure simulated intelligence rationale in a secluded way.

Model Conduct Tree
pgsql
Duplicate
Alter
Root
├── Grouping (Assault Choice)
│   ├── Really take a look at Foe in Reach?
│   ├── Move to Adversary
│   ├── Assault
├── Selector (Contingency plan)
      ├── Look for Adversary
      ├── Watch

✔ More adaptable than FSMs (utilized in present day game artificial intelligence).

✔ Can deal with complex NPC ways of behaving like secrecy, cooperation, and dynamic direction.

Could you like a model C++ execution of a conduct tree?

6. AI in Games

However uncommon continuously games, ML is utilized in:

✔ Versatile man-made intelligence (man-made intelligence gains from players) - Utilized in hustling games like Forza Skyline.

✔ Procedural computer based intelligence (Produces levels, ways of behaving powerfully) - Utilized in No Man's Sky.

✔ Support Learning (Self-learning man-made intelligence) - Utilized in AlphaGo.

Audio & Sound Effects in C++
Game Development ♪ 🎮

Audio cues and music make games vivid and locking in. In this aide, we'll cover:

✔ Playing audio effects and ambient sound

✔ Utilizing sound libraries like SDL2_mixer, FMOD, and OpenAL

✔ 3D positional sound for sensible soundscapes

1. Picking a Sound Library for C++

C++ doesn't have implicit sound help, so we utilize outside libraries:

Library	Best For	License
SDL2_mixer	Simple 2D sound (retro games, independent games)	Free (Zlib)
FMOD	AAA-quality sound (powerful music, enormous scope games)	Free (Non mainstream), Paid (Master)
OpenAL	3D positional sound (VR, encompass sound)	Open-source
irrKlang	Lightweight and simple to-use	Free for non-business use

2. Playing Audio cues with SDL2_mixer 🎵♪

SDL2_mixer is straightforward and extraordinary for 2D games.

Introducing SDL2_mixer
1️⃣ ▪ Download SDL2 and SDL2_mixer from libsdl.org
2️⃣ ▪ Introduce with vcpkg (Windows):

sh
Duplicate
Alter
vcpkg introduce sdl2-blender
3️⃣ ▪ Connection SDL2_mixer:

Linux: - lSDL2_mixer
Windows: Add SDL2_mixer.lib to your undertaking
Fundamental SDL2_mixer Model (Playing a Sound)
cpp
Duplicate
Alter
#incorporate <SDL2/SDL.h>
#incorporate <SDL2/SDL_mixer.h>

```
#incorporate <iostream>

int principal() {
  on the off chance that
(SDL_Init(SDL_INIT_AUDIO) < 0) {
    std::cerr << "SDL Init Blunder: " <<
SDL_GetError() << "\n";
    bring 1 back;
  }

  if             (Mix_OpenAudio(44100,
MIX_DEFAULT_FORMAT, 2, 2048) < 0) {
    std::cerr << "Mix_OpenAudio Blunder:
" << Mix_GetError() << "\n";
    bring 1 back;
  }

  Mix_Chunk*        sound        =
Mix_LoadWAV("jump.wav");
  if (!sound) {
    std::cerr << "Neglected to stack
sound: " << Mix_GetError() << "\n";
    bring 1 back;
  }
```

```cpp
    Mix_PlayChannel(- 1, sound, 0);//Play
the sound once
    SDL_Delay(2000);//Trust that sound
will play

    Mix_FreeChunk(sound);
    Mix_CloseAudio();
    SDL_Quit();
    bring 0 back;
}
```

✔ Extraordinary for playing basic audio effects like leaps, assaults, or blasts!

3. Playing Ambient sound 🎼

For circling music, we use Mix_PlayMusic().

cpp
Duplicate
Alter

```cpp
Mix_Music*        bgMusic        =
Mix_LoadMUS("background.mp3");
Mix_PlayMusic(bgMusic, - 1);// - 1 =
Circle until the end of time
```

✔ Upholds MP3, WAV, OGG designs
✔ Simple to circle and blur in/out

To respite or resume music:

```cpp
Duplicate
Alter
Mix_PauseMusic();//Delay
Mix_ResumeMusic();//Resume
Mix_HaltMusic();//Stop
```

4. 3D Positional Sound with OpenAL 🎧

For 3D games, we want positional sound (sound changes in light of area). OpenAL is perfect for this.

Introducing OpenAL
Linux: sudo able introduce libopenal-dev
Windows: Download from openal.org
Essential OpenAL Model (3D Sound Situating)

```cpp
Duplicate
Alter
#incorporate <AL/al.h>
#incorporate <AL/alc.h>
#incorporate <iostream>
```

```
int principal() {
  ALCdevice*         gadget        =
alcOpenDevice(nullptr);//Open    default
sound gadget
  if (!gadget) {
    std::cerr  <<  "Neglected  to  open
OpenAL device.\n";
    bring 1 back;
  }

  ALCcontext*        setting        =
alcCreateContext(device, nullptr);
  alcMakeContextCurrent(context);

  ALuint cradle, source;
  alGenBuffers(1, &buffer);
  alGenSources(1, &source);

  // Load  sound  information  (WAV
design expected for effortlessness)
  // Expect "sound.wav" is preloaded into
cushion

  alSourcei(source,         AL_BUFFER,
support);
```

```
  alSource3f(source, AL_POSITION, 0.0f,
0.0f, - 5.0f);//3D position (behind
audience)
  alSourcePlay(source);

  // Trust that the sound will play

std::this_thread::sleep_for(std::chrono::se
conds(3));

  alDeleteSources(1, &source);
  alDeleteBuffers(1, &buffer);
  alcDestroyContext(context);
  alcCloseDevice(device);
  bring 0 back;
}
```

✔ Changes sound in view of position (valuable for FPS, hustling, or VR games).
✔ 3D soundscape (strides sound stronger when closer, calmer when far).

5. Involving FMOD for AAA Sound 🎤

FMOD is utilized in games like GTA, Destruction, and The Witcher.

Introducing FMOD

1️ ▪ Download FMOD Center Programming interface from fmod.com

2️ ▪ Concentrate and connection fmod.lib to your undertaking

FMOD Model (Unique Music Framework)

cpp

Duplicate

Alter

```cpp
#incorporate <fmod.hpp>
#incorporate <iostream>

int primary() {
  FMOD::System* framework;
  FMOD::Sound* sound;
  FMOD::System_Create(&system);
  framework              >init(512,
FMOD_INIT_NORMAL, nullptr);

  framework
>createSound("battle_music.mp3",
FMOD_LOOP_NORMAL, nullptr, &sound);
  framework >playSound(sound, nullptr,
bogus, nullptr);
```

```
    std::cout << "Playing music...\n";

std::this_thread::sleep_for(std::chrono::se
conds(10));

    sound->release();
    framework >close();
    framework >release();
    bring 0 back;
}
```
✔ FMOD upholds dynamic impacts (reverb, channels, ongoing blending).

6. Audio effects Best Practices 🎮

✅ Utilize short, compacted sound records for audio effects (WAV, OGG).

✅ Preload and reuse sounds to keep away from slack.

✅ Utilize positional sound for authenticity in 3D games.

✅ Change volume and pitch for assortment (e.g., somewhat unique discharge sounds).

✅ Utilize dynamic blending for vivid sound (duck ambient sound when blasts occur).

7. Synopsis and Subsequent stages

♪ SDL2_mixer - Straightforward and simple for 2D games.

🎧 OpenAL - 3D positional sound for vivid universes.

✏️ FMOD - AAA sound quality with dynamic impacts.

Optimization & Performance Tuning in C++ Game Development 🎮🕹️

Upgrading a game is vital for smooth ongoing interaction, decreased load times, and effective memory use. This guide covers:

✔ Code improvement procedures
✔ Memory the board best practices
✔ Multithreading for execution
✔ Profiling instruments for troubleshooting bottlenecks

1. Code Advancement Strategies 🚀

1.1 Utilize Productive Information Designs

Picking the right information design can definitely further develop execution.

Task   Better Decision
Quick lookup std::unordered_map   (O(1) versus O(log n) for std::map)
Speedy   supplement/remove   std::list (connected list)

Quick iteration   std::vector
(preferred reserve territory over std::list)
1.2 Stay away from Costly Activities in Circles
🚫 Awful:

```cpp
Duplicate
Alter
for (int I = 0; I < objects.size(); i++) {
  std::cout << "Handling: " << objects[i].name << "\n";//Unoptimized
}
```

✔️ Better:

```cpp
Duplicate
Alter
for (const auto& obj : objects) {//Use range-based for circle
  std::cout << "Handling: " << obj.name << "\n";
}
```

✔ Lessens superfluous calls to .size() and further develops store effectiveness.

2. Memory The board Best Practices 🖫
2.1 Keep away from Memory Holes with Brilliant Pointers

Utilizing crude pointers (new/erase) can cause memory spills. Utilize brilliant pointers all things considered.

🚫 Awful:

```cpp
Duplicate
Alter
GameObject* obj = new GameObject();
erase obj;//Chance of neglecting erase →
Memory spill!
```

✅ Better (Savvy Pointer Model):

```cpp
Duplicate
Alter
#incorporate <memory>
std::unique_ptr<GameObject>    obj    =
std::make_unique<GameObject>();
```

✔ Consequently deallocates memory when out of degree.

2.2 Lessen Load Portions with Item Pools

Assigning objects on the pile much of the time causes discontinuity. Utilize an Article Pool all things being equal.

🚀 Model: Article Pooling

```cpp
Duplicate
Alter
class ObjectPool {
  std::vector<GameObject*> pool;
public:
  GameObject* GetObject() {
    if (!pool.empty()) {
      GameObject* obj = pool.back();
      pool.pop_back();
      return obj;
    }
    return new GameObject();
  }

  void ReturnObject(GameObject* obj) {
    pool.push_back(obj);
  }
```

};
✔ Reuses objects as opposed to dispensing new ones more than once.

3. Multithreading for Execution ▢
Game motors utilize various strings for:
✔ Delivering (Illustrations)
✔ Physical science Recreation
✔ Computer based intelligence Pathfinding

3.1 Utilizing std::thread for Multithreading
cpp
Duplicate
Alter

```cpp
#incorporate <iostream>
#incorporate <thread>

void LoadAssets() {
  std::cout << "Stacking resources in background...\n";
}

int fundamental() {
```

```cpp
    std::thread
assetThread(LoadAssets);//Run          in
discrete string
    assetThread.join();//Sit      tight      for
fruition
    std::cout << "Resources loaded!\n";
    bring 0 back;
}
```

✔ Further develops execution by running assignments in equal.

3.2 String Pooling (Proficient Multi-stringing)

Rather than making/obliterating strings each edge, utilize a string pool.

```cpp
cpp
Duplicate
Alter
#incorporate <queue>
#incorporate <vector>
#incorporate <thread>
#incorporate <functional>

class ThreadPool {
    std::vector<std::thread> laborers;
```

```cpp
  std::queue<std::function<void()>>
undertakings;
public:
  ThreadPool(size_t numThreads) {
    for (size_t I = 0; I < numThreads; ++i)
{
      workers.emplace_back([this] {
        while (!tasks.empty()) {
          auto task = tasks.front();
          tasks.pop();
          task();
        }
      });
    }
  }

  void      AddTask(std::function<void()>
task) {
    tasks.push(task);
  }

  void JoinAll() {
    for (auto& t : laborers) t.join();
  }
};
```

✔ Reuses strings as opposed to making new ones each time.

4. Profiling and Investigating Execution Bottlenecks ⏱⏳

Use profilers to identify slow code:

✔ Visual Studio Profiler - Worked in, simple for Windows

✔ gprof - GNU profiler for Linux/macOS

✔ Valgrind - Finds memory spills

✔ Remotery - Ongoing central processor/GPU profiler

4.1 Utilizing std::chrono for Essential Timing

cpp

Duplicate

Alter

```cpp
#incorporate <iostream>
#incorporate <chrono>

void ExpensiveFunction() {
    for (int I = 0; I < 1e6; i++);
}

int fundamental() {
```

```cpp
    auto            start            =
std::chrono::high_resolution_clock::now()
;

    ExpensiveFunction();

    auto            end            =
std::chrono::high_resolution_clock::now()
;
    std::cout << "Execution time: "
        <<
std::chrono::duration_cast<std::chrono::m
illiseconds>(end - start).count()
        << " ms\n";
    bring 0 back;
}
```

✔ Assists measure execution with timing to track down bottlenecks.

5. Improving Designs and Delivering 🎨
5.1 Use Item Clustering

Sending one draw call for every article is wasteful. All things considered, bunch protests together.

🚫 Awful:

```cpp
Duplicate
Alter
for (auto& sprite : sprites) {
  RenderSprite(sprite);//Different   draw
calls = Awful
}
```

✅ Better:

```cpp
Duplicate
Alter
BatchRender(sprites);//One           draw
require various items = Quicker
```

✔ Diminishes computer chip GPU correspondence above.

5.2 Utilize Level of Detail (LOD)

Render low-poly models for far off objects to save GPU power.

Distance	Model Type
Close	High-poly
Mid-range	Medium-poly
Far	Low-poly

6. Lessening Burden Times 🚀
6.1 Offbeat Resource Stacking

Rather than freezing the game while stacking resources, load them behind the scenes.

✅ Load Surfaces Nonconcurrently

cpp
Duplicate
Alter
```cpp
std::thread LoadThread(LoadTextures);
LoadThread.detach();//Run in foundation
```
✔ Forestalls faltering and keeps the game responsive.

7. Rundown and Following stages

✅ Upgrade circles and utilize effective information structures

✅ Lessen memory allotments with object pooling

✅ Use multithreading for physical science, simulated intelligence, and resource stacking

✓ Profile the game utilizing devices like gprof or Visual Studio Profiler

✓ Cluster draw calls and use LOD for designs

Building a Complete Game Project in C++ 🎮🚀

Uniting every one of the ideas, we should stroll through the most common way of building a total game in C++! This guide covers:

✔ Setting up your venture

✔ Game engineering and construction

✔ Executing center game mechanics

✔ Adding designs, sound, and info taking care of

✔ Upgrading and cleaning the game

1. Setting Up the Venture 🛠️
1.1 Picking the Right System

C++ offers a few libraries and motors:

Structure/Engine	Best For	Difficulty
SDL2	2D games, straightforward projects	Beginner
SFML	2D games, multimedia	Beginner
OpenGL + GLFW	Custom 3D motor development	Advanced

Incredible Motor (C++)   AAA-quality
3D games   Intermediate
Godot (C++ Backend)   Open-source
2D/3D engine   Intermediate
For this aide, we'll utilize SDL2 (Basic
DirectMedia Layer) as it's lightweight and
simple to set up.

1.2 Introducing SDL2 (for Windows, Linux, Macintosh)
Windows (Utilizing vcpkg)
sh
Duplicate
Alter
vcpkg introduce sdl2 sdl2-picture sdl2-blender sdl2-ttf
Linux (Ubuntu/Debian)
sh
Duplicate
Alter
sudo able introduce libsdl2-dev libsdl2-picture dev libsdl2-blender dev libsdl2-ttf-dev
Macintosh (Homemade libation)
sh
Duplicate

Alter

mix introduce sdl2 sdl2_image sdl2_mixer sdl2_ttf

2. Game Engineering and Center Circle 🔲🔲

2.1 Fundamental Game Circle

Each game follows a circle structure:

1🔲 ▪ Handle input

2🔲 ▪ Update game state (development, material science, artificial intelligence, and so on.)

3🔲 ▪ Render designs

cpp
Duplicate
Alter

```cpp
#incorporate <SDL2/SDL.h>
#incorporate <iostream>

bool isRunning = valid;
SDL_Window* window = nullptr;
SDL_Renderer* renderer = nullptr;

void InitGame() {
    SDL_Init(SDL_INIT_VIDEO);
```

```cpp
  window   =   SDL_CreateWindow("C++
Game",    SDL_WINDOWPOS_CENTERED,
SDL_WINDOWPOS_CENTERED, 800, 600,
0);
  renderer                        =
SDL_CreateRenderer(window,   -    1,
SDL_RENDERER_ACCELERATED);
}

void HandleInput() {
  SDL_Event occasion;
  while (SDL_PollEvent(&event)) {
    on the off chance that (event.type ==
SDL_QUIT) {
      isRunning = misleading;
    }
  }
}

void Update() {
  // Game rationale (e.g., development,
impact recognition)
}

void Render() {
```

```
   SDL_SetRenderDrawColor(renderer,   0,
0, 0, 255);
   SDL_RenderClear(renderer);

   // Render game articles here

   SDL_RenderPresent(renderer);
}

void Cleanup() {
   SDL_DestroyRenderer(renderer);
   SDL_DestroyWindow(window);
   SDL_Quit();
}

int primary() {
   InitGame();

   while (isRunning) {
     HandleInput();
     Update();
     Render();
   }

   Cleanup();
   bring 0 back;
```

}

✔ Makes a straightforward window and game circle.

3. Carrying out Center Game Mechanics 🎮

3.1 Player Development

We should move a person utilizing the bolt keys.

```cpp
Duplicate
Alter
int playerX = 400, playerY = 300;

void HandleInput() {
    SDL_Event occasion;
    while (SDL_PollEvent(&event)) {
        on the off chance that (event.type ==
SDL_QUIT) isRunning = bogus;

        const       Uint8*       keys       =
SDL_GetKeyboardState(NULL);
        in       the       event       that
(keys[SDL_SCANCODE_LEFT]) playerX - =
5;
```

```
    in      the      event      that
(keys[SDL_SCANCODE_RIGHT])    playerX
+= 5;
    in      the      event      that
(keys[SDL_SCANCODE_UP]) playerY - = 5;
    in      the      event      that
(keys[SDL_SCANCODE_DOWN])    playerY
+= 5;
  }
}

void Render() {
  SDL_SetRenderDrawColor(renderer,   0,
0, 0, 255);
  SDL_RenderClear(renderer);

  SDL_Rect player = {playerX, playerY, 50,
50};
  SDL_SetRenderDrawColor(renderer,
255, 0, 0, 255);
  SDL_RenderFillRect(renderer, &player);

  SDL_RenderPresent(renderer);
}
```
✔ Bolt keys move a red square (player).

4. Adding Designs and Sound 🎨🔊
4.1 Stacking Surfaces

cpp
Duplicate
Alter

```cpp
SDL_Texture* LoadTexture(const char* filePath) {
  SDL_Surface* surface = SDL_LoadBMP(filePath);
  SDL_Texture* surface = SDL_CreateTextureFromSurface(renderer, surface);
  SDL_FreeSurface(surface);
  bring surface back;
}

SDL_Texture* playerTexture = LoadTexture("player.bmp");

void Render() {
  SDL_RenderClear(renderer);
  SDL_Rect dest = {playerX, playerY, 50, 50};
  SDL_RenderCopy(renderer, playerTexture, Invalid, &dest);
  SDL_RenderPresent(renderer);
```

```
}
```

✔ Replaces the red square with a person sprite.

4.2 Adding Audio cues

Utilizing SDL2_mixer to play sounds:

```cpp
cpp
Duplicate
Alter
#incorporate <SDL2/SDL_mixer.h>

Mix_Chunk*        jumpSound        =
Mix_LoadWAV("jump.wav");

void HandleInput() {
  const       Uint8*       keys       =
SDL_GetKeyboardState(NULL);
  in       the       event       that
(keys[SDL_SCANCODE_SPACE]) {
    Mix_PlayChannel(-  1,  jumpSound,
0);//Play bounce sound
  }
}
```

✔ Squeezing SPACE plays a leap sound.

5. Crash Location and Physical science
⚡

5.1 Fundamental Square shape Impact
cpp
Duplicate
Alter

```cpp
bool CheckCollision(SDL_Rect a, SDL_Rect b) {
    return (a.x < b.x + b.w && a.x + a.w > b.x
&& a.y < b.y + b.h && a.y + a.h > b.y);
}
```

✔ Identifies assuming two square shapes cross-over.

5.2 Gravity and Bouncing
cpp
Duplicate
Alter

```cpp
float velocityY = 0;
bool isJumping = bogus;

void Update() {
    velocityY += 0.5f;//Gravity
    playerY += (int)velocityY;
```

```cpp
    on the off chance that (playerY >= 500)
{//Ground crash
        playerY = 500;
        velocityY = 0;
        isJumping = bogus;
    }
}

void HandleInput() {
    const        Uint8*        keys        =
SDL_GetKeyboardState(NULL);
    on      the      off      chance      that
(keys[SDL_SCANCODE_SPACE]          &&
!isJumping) {
        velocityY = - 10;//Bounce
        isJumping = valid;
    }
}
```

✔ Straightforward hopping physical science!

6. Enhancing and Cleaning the Game ☞
6.1 Utilizing Delta Time for Smoother Development
cpp
Duplicate

Alter
```
Uint32 lastFrameTime = 0;

void Update() {
  Uint32 currentFrame = SDL_GetTicks();
  float deltaTime = (currentFrame - lastFrameTime)/1000.0f;
  lastFrameTime = currentFrame;

  playerY += (int)(velocityY * deltaTime);
}
```
✔ Makes development steady across various edge rates.

6.2 Adding a Game State Framework

cpp
Duplicate
Alter
```
enum GameState { MENU, PLAYING, GAME_OVER };
GameState currentState = MENU;

void HandleInput() {
  if (currentState == MENU && SDL_GetKeyboardState(NULL)[SDL_SCANCODE_RETURN]) {
```

```
    currentState = PLAYING;
  }
}
```

✔ Makes different game states (Menu, Playing, Game Over).

7. Last Advances and Next Objectives 🚀

✅ Game circle, input taking care of, delivering

✅ Surfaces, audio effects, and material science

✅ Enhancement and smooth development

Conclusion: Mastering C++ for Game Development 🎮🚀

Uniting every one of the ideas, we should stroll through the most common way of building a total game in C++! This guide covers:

✔ Setting up your venture

✔ Game engineering and construction

✔ Executing center game mechanics

✔ Adding designs, sound, and info taking care of

✔ Upgrading and cleaning the game

1. Setting Up the Venture 🛠️

1.1 Picking the Right System

C++ offers a few libraries and motors:

Structure/Engine	Best For	Difficulty
SDL2	2D games, straightforward projects	Beginner
SFML	2D games, multimedia	Beginner
OpenGL + GLFW	Custom 3D motor development	Advanced

Incredible Motor (C++)   AAA-quality
3D games   Intermediate
Godot (C++ Backend)   Open-source
2D/3D engine   Intermediate
For this aide, we'll utilize SDL2 (Basic DirectMedia Layer) as it's lightweight and simple to set up.

1.2 Introducing SDL2 (for Windows, Linux, Macintosh)

Windows (Utilizing vcpkg)

sh

Duplicate

Alter

vcpkg introduce sdl2 sdl2-picture sdl2-blender sdl2-ttf

Linux (Ubuntu/Debian)

sh

Duplicate

Alter

sudo able introduce libsdl2-dev libsdl2-picture dev libsdl2-blender dev libsdl2-ttf-dev

Macintosh (Homemade libation)

sh

Duplicate

Alter

mix introduce sdl2 sdl2_image sdl2_mixer sdl2_ttf

2. Game Engineering and Center Circle 🞏🞏

2.1 Fundamental Game Circle

Each game follows a circle structure:

1🞏 ▪ Handle input

2🞏 ▪ Update game state (development, material science, artificial intelligence, and so on.)

3🞏 ▪ Render designs

cpp
Duplicate
Alter

```cpp
#incorporate <SDL2/SDL.h>
#incorporate <iostream>

bool isRunning = valid;
SDL_Window* window = nullptr;
SDL_Renderer* renderer = nullptr;

void InitGame() {
  SDL_Init(SDL_INIT_VIDEO);
```

```
  window    =    SDL_CreateWindow("C++
Game",    SDL_WINDOWPOS_CENTERED,
SDL_WINDOWPOS_CENTERED, 800, 600,
0);
  renderer                          =
SDL_CreateRenderer(window,    -    1,
SDL_RENDERER_ACCELERATED);
}

void HandleInput() {
  SDL_Event occasion;
  while (SDL_PollEvent(&event)) {
    on the off chance that (event.type ==
SDL_QUIT) {
      isRunning = misleading;
    }
  }
}

void Update() {
  // Game rationale (e.g., development,
impact recognition)
}

void Render() {
```

```
  SDL_SetRenderDrawColor(renderer,   0,
0, 0, 255);
  SDL_RenderClear(renderer);

  // Render game articles here

  SDL_RenderPresent(renderer);
}

void Cleanup() {
  SDL_DestroyRenderer(renderer);
  SDL_DestroyWindow(window);
  SDL_Quit();
}

int primary() {
  InitGame();

  while (isRunning) {
    HandleInput();
    Update();
    Render();
  }

  Cleanup();
  bring 0 back;
```

```
}
```
✔ Makes a straightforward window and game circle.

3. Carrying out Center Game Mechanics 🎮

3.1 Player Development

We should move a person utilizing the bolt keys.

```cpp
cpp
Duplicate
Alter
int playerX = 400, playerY = 300;

void HandleInput() {
  SDL_Event occasion;
  while (SDL_PollEvent(&event)) {
    on the off chance that (event.type == SDL_QUIT) isRunning = bogus;

    const Uint8* keys = SDL_GetKeyboardState(NULL);
    in the event that (keys[SDL_SCANCODE_LEFT]) playerX - = 5;
```

```
    in        the       event        that
(keys[SDL_SCANCODE_RIGHT])    playerX
+= 5;
    in        the       event        that
(keys[SDL_SCANCODE_UP]) playerY - = 5;
    in        the       event        that
(keys[SDL_SCANCODE_DOWN])    playerY
+= 5;
  }
}

void Render() {
  SDL_SetRenderDrawColor(renderer,   0,
0, 0, 255);
  SDL_RenderClear(renderer);

  SDL_Rect player = {playerX, playerY, 50,
50};
  SDL_SetRenderDrawColor(renderer,
255, 0, 0, 255);
  SDL_RenderFillRect(renderer, &player);

  SDL_RenderPresent(renderer);
}
```
✔ Bolt keys move a red square (player).

4. Adding Designs and Sound 🎬🔊
4.1 Stacking Surfaces

cpp
Duplicate
Alter

```cpp
SDL_Texture* LoadTexture(const char* filePath) {
    SDL_Surface* surface = SDL_LoadBMP(filePath);
    SDL_Texture* surface = SDL_CreateTextureFromSurface(renderer, surface);
    SDL_FreeSurface(surface);
    bring surface back;
}

SDL_Texture* playerTexture = LoadTexture("player.bmp");

void Render() {
    SDL_RenderClear(renderer);
    SDL_Rect dest = {playerX, playerY, 50, 50};
    SDL_RenderCopy(renderer, playerTexture, Invalid, &dest);
    SDL_RenderPresent(renderer);
```

}
✔ Replaces the red square with a person sprite.

4.2 Adding Audio cues
Utilizing SDL2_mixer to play sounds:

```cpp
Duplicate
Alter
#incorporate <SDL2/SDL_mixer.h>

Mix_Chunk*        jumpSound        =
Mix_LoadWAV("jump.wav");

void HandleInput() {
  const      Uint8*      keys      =
SDL_GetKeyboardState(NULL);
  in      the      event      that
(keys[SDL_SCANCODE_SPACE]) {
    Mix_PlayChannel(-  1,  jumpSound,
0);//Play bounce sound
  }
}
```
✔ Squeezing SPACE plays a leap sound.

5. Crash Location and Physical science
⚡

5.1 Fundamental Square shape Impact
cpp
Duplicate
Alter

```cpp
bool CheckCollision(SDL_Rect a, SDL_Rect b) {
    return (a.x < b.x + b.w && a.x + a.w > b.x && a.y < b.y + b.h && a.y + a.h > b.y);
}
```

✔ Identifies assuming two square shapes cross-over.

5.2 Gravity and Bouncing
cpp
Duplicate
Alter

```cpp
float velocityY = 0;
bool isJumping = bogus;

void Update() {
    velocityY += 0.5f;//Gravity
    playerY += (int)velocityY;
```

on the off chance that (playerY >= 500) {//Ground crash
```
    playerY = 500;
    velocityY = 0;
    isJumping = bogus;
  }
}

void HandleInput() {
  const       Uint8*      keys      =
SDL_GetKeyboardState(NULL);
  on     the     off     chance     that
(keys[SDL_SCANCODE_SPACE]      &&
!isJumping) {
    velocityY = - 10;//Bounce
    isJumping = valid;
  }
}
```
✔ Straightforward hopping physical science!

6. Enhancing and Cleaning the Game ⚙

6.1 Utilizing Delta Time for Smoother Development

cpp

Duplicate

Alter
```
Uint32 lastFrameTime = 0;

void Update() {
  Uint32 currentFrame = SDL_GetTicks();
  float deltaTime = (currentFrame - lastFrameTime)/1000.0f;
  lastFrameTime = currentFrame;

  playerY += (int)(velocityY * deltaTime);
}
```
✔ Makes development steady across various edge rates.

6.2 Adding a Game State Framework
cpp
Duplicate
Alter
```
enum GameState { MENU, PLAYING, GAME_OVER };
GameState currentState = MENU;

void HandleInput() {
  if (currentState == MENU && SDL_GetKeyboardState(NULL)[SDL_SCANCODE_RETURN]) {
```

```
    currentState = PLAYING;
  }
}
```

✔ Makes different game states (Menu, Playing, Game Over).

7. Last Advances and Next Objectives 🚀

✅ Game circle, input taking care of, delivering

✅ Surfaces, audio effects, and material science

✅ Enhancement and smooth development.